NO NONSENSE EXAM SUCCESS

By

Tony Ray

All rights reserved.

No part of this book may be produced or transmitted in any form, or by any means, electronic or mechanical, including photocopying, recording by any information storage and retrieval system, without written permission from the author, except for the inclusion of brief quotations in a review.

All rights reserved.
Copyright © 2013 Tony Ray

Dedicated to Tracey, Daniel and Stephanie.
Thanks for the love, support and editing skills.

CONTENTS

INTRODUCTION

SECTION ONE: READY TO WIN
1. Confidence building techniques
2. First gear
3. Second gear
4. Third gear
5. Turbo boost
6. Flick off!
7. Aim at your target
8. Reducing Exam Stress
9. Relaxation techniques
10. Thinking time
11. Techniques for Creative Thinking

SECTION TWO: SKILLS FOR THE JOB
12. Organising your revision
13. Adapt and prioritise
14. Speed reading
15. Efficient Reading
16. Taking Notes
17. Reducing your notes
18. Breaking down your subject
19. Don't like your subject? Do this.
20. Pro active learning

SECTION THREE: MEMORISE EVERYTHING

21. Memory and Recall
22. Memory lists
23. Memorising difficult words
24. Using people as memory aids
25. The acting or music learning technique
26. Memorise every note
27. Another example
28. Past papers
29. Panic stations!
30. The day of the exam
31. Forget it!

APPENDIX 1

APPENDIX 2

INTRODUCTION

An exam is an event, just as much as a boxing match, or a race; an Olympic event for the mind. To be successful, you need to prepare and train for it. Importantly, the preparation has to be right, so you can be on top form on the day. This eBook is going to take you through the techniques you need to pass exams and gain top marks. You will learn everything you need to know, in about an hour. The techniques I am going to describe, changed a persistent exam failure like me, into someone who regularly achieved first degree level exam pass marks at University. This exam revision approach is very simple, and extremely effective. Together, we're going to make you an exam champion.

For many people who struggle with exams, the problem is often that they don't have an effective revision strategy. Not knowing how to revise, as well as a heavy workload or exam nerves, can all have a negative impact on exam performance. I struggled with all those problems, and I was probably worse than most. In one exam I was so stressed, I couldn't write my name on the exam paper until half way through the exam, because I couldn't remember my surname!

Like many geeks, I was top of my class in school in almost every subject, except sport. However, I couldn't pass an exam to save my life. I got excellent marks in class, and failed exams miserably. It was so frustrating. I would put hours in doing homework, only to see the kids who messed about in class get better exam results than I did.

I enjoyed school, and I was determined to do well, so I stayed on in the sixth form. In theory, I shouldn't have. My exam marks weren't good enough, but I managed to persuade the school that seeing as I was good at homework and class work, that I should be able to manage A levels. The same thing happened again, though. I got good marks in class, and one A level grade E. I think they had to toss a coin to decide whether I got it or not.

I decided at that point, I was never going to do another exam as long as I live. Unfortunately, as luck would have it, it was a time of high unemployment when I left school. I took the first job I could get, which turned out to be as a trainee in the optical profession. Guess what? There were exams to pass. The training involved a three year, weekly correspondence course, and a final exam, both theory and practical. I got excellent marks on the course work, passed the practical, failed the theory. I retook the exam about eight or ten times over the course of the next ten years, and still didn't pass. Fortunately, it turned out that I was actually good at managing people, so I eventually achieved a reasonable living, but I could have achieved more, and achieved it earlier, had I been able to pass exams.

Twenty years later, as a means of improving my job prospects, I took Microsoft Office exams. I passed one, and failed four. Same old problem.

Later in life than most, I got the opportunity to study full time for a degree at university. I loved university from the first minute. As soon as I attended my first lecture, I knew it was for me. Until five minutes before the end. That was when the lecturer informed us that we would be tested by written assignment, and by an end of term exam. You could have heard my jaw hit the floor. It never entered my mind there would be exams. I thought they were a thing of the past.

In the run up to the exams, I tried my best to revise, not really knowing what to do. I attended a study skills class at university, which was excellent, but I still felt the information was too generalised, which it had to be because of the different student learning styles. I still didn't know specifically what to do. Three weeks before the exam, I just accepted that I would probably fail, and the best I could hope for was to make sure that I made up for it in the assignments.

Then I had two bits of luck. Two weeks before the exam, I discovered how to structure my revision, and I also discovered memory techniques. The techniques were easy to learn, and I soon picked them up. I passed with a mark of 70%, the equivalent of a first class degree pass. My previous average mark in an exam had been about 24%. What's more, this time I was ninth in a class of ninety six, not near the bottom, like I usually was. I was in the top ten per cent, and I was ecstatic about that. I had never done anywhere near as well as that before.

However, it made me think. Out of those ninety six students who took the exam, there were likely to be somewhere near fifty per cent of students, who had struggled with exams as I had done. Otherwise they would have got higher marks. That's excluding those who perhaps could have achieved better grades, but didn't put the work in. There are always a few of those. When I thought back to the study skills classes, I remember being surprised by how many third year university students were in the class. Some students had obviously not got their exam problem sorted, even by their third year.

Since that time, using the same techniques, I continued to achieve First level pass rates in each of the remaining exams I took while at university. In my last year, in my last exam, I achieved my best ever marks; well within first class degree standard. I also lost my fear of exams.

I have added to, and improved the strategies and techniques which brought me success at last, and I've now put together them in this eBook. The techniques are amazingly simple, need no special knowledge or skill, and everyone can do them, as long as you have an imagination. It's likely that you will only need an hour or so to read this eBook. What you will learn during the hour, should be useful to you in your daily life, in your career, but particularly when you take exams.

These techniques should be useful for whatever type of work you go into. If you want to be an engineer, or a hairdresser, or even an engineer who cuts hair on the side, some of the techniques we'll talk about, will hopefully give you an edge over people who don't know them. They will help you learn and retain information. That could improve your potential job or promotion prospects.

These techniques work just as well with Maths, Science and Languages, as well as other subjects. At the end of this eBook are two appendices with examples for Maths and Music.

Some of you may already do well in exams. You might feel you don't need any help. However, I would recommend you not to pass up the chance to learn these useful skills. Just in case. They may just add the one or two marks you might need to get that higher grade. I have taught these techniques to other people, and now they, like me, are just as confident of achieving success in exams, as they are with course work.

Over the next hour or so, you will learn:

Confidence building techniques
Stress reduction techniques
Highly effective memory techniques
Effective note taking techniques, which aid memory and recall
Strategies for dealing with problem subjects
Effective organisational strategies for exams
The importance of thinking time
Problem solving techniques

Techniques for creative thinking
Effective study techniques
…..and a few more beside.

Learn the techniques in the order they are written, as one technique builds on the previous one. The idea first of all, is to give you confidence that you can achieve. We'll then work on controlling, and removing stress. Then we'll move on to note taking to improve your memory. By the end of the eBook, you will be able to remember vast amounts of information, and recall it when you need it. By the time you've read this eBook, you will be ready for whatever exams throw at you. Get ready to achieve top marks!

1. Confidence building techniques

One of the main reasons people become stressed or anxious, is when they feel they're not in control. So, the first section is about taking control – of yourself.

Let's look into the future. I want you to close your eyes and imagine that you have already taken your exams, and it's results day. Perhaps your friends or family are with you, or both. Imagine you have opened the results and you cannot believe what you see. You've passed, and what's more, the grades are fantastic. Even if you believe at the moment that won't happen, I want you to imagine that it does. Use your imagination. Imagine you've passed your exams. Passed them with far better marks than you ever thought possible. All those people who may have doubted you, or put pressure on you, and that may include yourself, are amazed at what you've achieved. Imagine how it feels. How excited are you? What are you doing? Are you jumping up and down, perhaps hugging your friends and family? You really have done fantastically well. Imagine the reaction of your friends and family. How proud they are of you. What do you feel like inside? Use your senses to make your imagination more real. What are the sounds and the scents around you? Really feel what you've achieved.

I want you to keep hold of that image, that feeling, and come back to it every now and again, because that is your target. That is what you are aiming for – that feeling of success, of achievement, of passing your exams with fantastic marks. So, let's make it happen.

2. *First gear*

Let's get you in the right frame of mind to be successful. First of all, I'd like you to stand up. Close your eyes, and imagine that standing in front of you, is the most confident person you know, or have ever seen. It might be a parent or a teacher. It might be a pop star, or a footballer. Imagine them standing directly in front of you. Now, I want you imagine that you have the ability to float into their body. Go ahead, float into their body. Become them. Like an actor takes on a character. If you're struggling to think of someone confident, imagine yourself as a comic book hero, perhaps the mighty god Thor. Someone who can do anything they want. How do they stand, how do they feel? Take on their persona. Imagine you are that person. What thoughts are going through their mind? What are you experiencing from their senses? Imagine that you are now feeling their confidence.

Okay. Relax. Take, an imaginary step back. Go back to being yourself. Notice the difference, between how you feel normally, and the way it felt to be the more confident person. How did your posture change, when you became the more confident person? Perhaps you stood more upright, felt taller. You stood straight. Head held high.

Let's try it again. Become that confident person again. Float into their body. Stand how they stand. Imagine the confidence oozing from every pore.

3. Second gear

Right. You're in the confident persons body. Look ahead. I want you to imagine that standing in front of you, is someone who is ten times more confident than the confident person whose body you have floated into. Look at how they stand. Float into their body. Become them. How does that feel? Imagine. Ten times more confident than your confident hero. This person is capable of doing anything at all they set their minds to. Assume their posture. Stand how they stand. Feel the confidence flowing through them. Look around you, and take in what it is like to see as a ten times more confident person. Imagine what their senses are telling them. Now, imagine that person is you. You are the person who is ten times more confident than your confident hero. Look around, and feel what that feels like. Knowing you can be successful at whatever you try. How does that feel? Good eh?

Close your eyes again. This time take two imaginary steps back. First step, back to the body of your confident hero. Then, back to your original self. Relax. Breathe slowly and gently. Keep your eyes closed.

4. Third gear

Now, float two imaginary steps forward into the ten times more confident body. Then, take one step back into the confident hero you first thought of. Step back once again to yourself. Can you feel what happens every time you float forward or step back? You change your confidence levels, just by using your imagination. Changing your posture makes you more confident. Now, that also means that you can change yourself into whatever type of mood you want, just by following this simple technique. If you feel a bit down in the dumps, think about someone who is generally happy. Change your posture, become them, or someone ten times happier than them. Use the techniques you have just learned to become ten times happier as yourself. You can change your state of mind, as simply as that. Use this technique for any situation where you need to feel confident or positive.

5. Turbo boost

To reinforce that feeling of confidence, I want you to think of your favourite colour. Got it? Next, think of your favourite number, and finally, your favourite song. Close your eyes, and see your favourite colour, and your favourite number. Choose a song which brings back good memories for you. Imagine you hear your favourite song, or even hum it to yourself. I want you to use these three things as your anchor points. Every time you see your favourite colour, or your favourite number, or hear or hum your favourite song, you will feel more confident. These are little reminders you can achieve whatever you want to; that you are in control. Every time you see or hear these anchor points, you will feel that extra confidence, and it will show, in your posture, and your happiness. It will make you smile. If you need a quick boost, listen to your favourite song on your music player.

6. Flick off!

Occasionally, you might have a tiny devil on your shoulder, telling you not to do something, or that you can't do something. Imagine him sitting there, whispering in your ear. On your other shoulder, imagine there is a tiny person who is always positive. This little positive voice on the other shoulder, is telling you that you can do whatever you put your mind to. So what do you do? Easy. Flick the little negative devil off your shoulder. Give him a really good flick. Send him flying off into space. Then shake hands with the positive tiny person, or pat him on the head. The little devil will get the message. You are the boss, you are in control, and you choose to succeed.

7. Take aim

Set yourself a target for your exams. What mark are you aiming for, realistically? Is your target easily within reach? If it is very easily within your capability, is your target too low? If you put the work in, could you achieve a better grade?

I wanted to be a teacher when I was younger. It never crossed my mind that I would do anything else, and I was fully committed to it. That was until a teacher, who I really admired, said that he thought I would be "too quiet" to be a teacher myself. It was certainly true that I was quite shy in those days. However, his comment changed my thinking immediately.

As I respected him, I believed he must be right. My mindset altered, and I completely lost my sense of what direction I wanted my life to take. I stumbled along for years, not really knowing what I wanted to do. Life tends to happen to you when you don't have a target to aim for, rather than you taking charge of what happens. Writing is my passion now, and I feel that I'm back on track again.

You may feel that you don't need a target to succeed. That's fine, many people achieve success without one. However, it is less likely that you will hit any target, if you don't know what the target is. Having something to aim for, can help you stay focussed on what you want to achieve. If you have a target in mind, stick to it, whatever might happen to throw you off course.

If you had all the money in the world, and you could do whatever you want, what would you choose? Now, given the fact that you are likely to have to work to earn money, is it possible that you could do what you chose in the last question for a living? It would be great if you could do something you love, and earn a living from it. Would you need qualifications to be able to do your dream job, or live your dream lifestyle? Most jobs need some kind of skill or qualification, especially if you are going to earn a decent living at it. If you had to plan to get that dream lifestyle, what do you think it would take for you to achieve it? As an exercise; briefly write out a plan for what you want to do with your life, and what you might need to achieve it.

Where would you start? What qualifications or experience might you need? What are the least number of steps you can take to achieve your goal? Set yourself small achievable goals, rather than large difficult to hit targets.

Every now and again, these are questions you should ask yourself. You stand a much better chance of achieving your goals (if you are targeting your ideal job or lifestyle), if you have an idea of the path that needs to be taken, and stick to it, even in the face of setbacks.

8. Reducing exam stress

Regular exercise is a great way to alleviate stress and improve your chances of getting a good nights sleep in the lead up to an exam, but there are also other simple techniques you can use.

I want you to look into the future again. This time, imagine you're in the exam hall, sitting the exam. Imagine you are nervous, a bit apprehensive.

Now, imagine you are watching yourself from above, on a CCTV screen. See yourself looking at the exam paper, waiting to turn it over. Imagine at the bottom of the imaginary CCTV screen are two control dials. The one on the right, is to turn up the colour. It makes colours more vivid and intense. The other is to make the image move towards or away from you.. If you turn the right hand dial to the right, the image on the screen, the colour, and the feelings you feel, become more intense. Turn the colour up on the right hand dial. See the colours become brighter, the intensity of the picture becomes stronger. You may feel yourself becoming more anxious. Now turn the dial the opposite way. Feel the intensity drop. Lower it further. If you want to, you can get rid of the colour altogether, and just make it black and white.

Change the left hand dial to the right to move the image closer to you. As you move the image towards you, feel how the intensity and your anxiety increases. Turn the dial to the left. The image moves away and anxiety decreases.

Adjust both dials until you feel the image move closer and the colour intensify. Can you feel your anxiety increase? Take control, and turn the dials in the opposite direction. The image moves away, and the brightness decreases. Adjust the dials so you have the colour intensity, and the position of the image, just where you want it. Feel the stress and anxiety drain away.

Try it once more. Turn the dials to the right again. See the colour intensify and the image move closer. When it gets too much, turn the dials to the left again, and the anxiety eases. You could get rid of the colour completely if you wish. In fact, I want you to make the picture black and white by turning the dial to the left. Imagine that you can take hold of that image on the screen with your left hand. I want you to grab hold of the picture, squeeze it, crush it. Put it in your right hand, and throw it as far as you can. Can you feel the difference? You can control your anxiety levels, simply by using your imagination.

These are simple techniques for controlling your stress levels in whatever circumstances you find yourself in. They are not like hypnosis, so you are never in a trance. Just the force of your imagination can work for you. By using these imaginary dials, you set your levels at a level that is comfortable for you. There may be a time when you need to be more motivated and direct. You might find increasing the intensity and image position gives that extra bit of drive and energy. Just alter the dials until you get the correct level.

9. Relaxation techniques

Let's concentrate on relaxation for a few minutes. You probably know that by controlling your breathing, you can relax yourself. So let's do that. Breathe in slowly, and gently, for a slow count of four. Now hold your breath for a count of four. Breathe out slowly, and gently, for a count of four, and hold your breath again for a count of four. Do that four times. Breathe in slowly, hold, breathe out slowly, hold. You should now find yourself in a relaxed state. Not only that, but you may find yourself much more aware of your surroundings. More alert.

Another technique is Mindful Breathing. Sit and make yourself comfortable. Close your eyes. Pay attention to your breathing. Feel your abdomen inflate slightly, like a balloon, as you breathe in gently. Notice the difference as your abdomen deflates as you breathe out. Thoughts will come into your mind, but let them flow out again, and concentrate on your breathing. If you hear sounds, or feel emotions, simply relax and concentrate on your breathing. If you notice your mind drifting away from your breathing, simply bring it back. Don't analyse or follow any thoughts that come into your mind. It's okay for them to be there, but for now, just bring your mind back to your breathing. This technique will take the edge off any anxiety, nervousness or even anger, you may feel.

These techniques are not only good for relaxation, but also for preparing yourself for study. Just in the way that a musician, or a sports person, may get themselves ready for a gig or an event. Try one of these techniques before you go into class next time. It will help improve your oxygen flow, and should help improve your concentration.

10. Thinking time

One of the things you need when you study, is thinking time. You will find, if you go on to higher education, that you'll be encouraged to take the time to think about what you are studying. So, you may write part of an essay, leave it for a day or two, think about it, talk to other people, and come back to it. Thinking time is important. Go for a walk, or perhaps just sit in a comfortable chair and relax. Find yourself a place where the ideas flow freely. For some strange reason, I used to get loads of great essay ideas in the shower, but not the bath. Wherever you find best for you, allow yourself to just think. No falling asleep when you should be thinking!

11. Techniques for creative thinking

You might find that there are times when you find yourself short of ideas, so this technique is useful. Simply relax in a chair, or on your bed, and stare at a point on the ceiling. Empty your mind of all your thoughts. Let your mind become completely empty. Don't think of anything. Relax. Let thoughts enter your mind naturally, and easily. At first, this can be difficult to do. You may have so many things going on in your mind that it is difficult to let go, but practice this exercise, and let the creative side of your brain take over for a while, and see what it comes up with. Often the creative side of your brain, and your practical side, are in competition with each other. The practical side usually wins, because it has to get you through the day. Occasionally though, you need the creative side to kick in, to help you find the solution to a problem.

You can also access the creative side of your brain by writing quickly with your wrong hand. Try it when you get the chance. If you are right handed, write your name quickly with your left hand ten times, without stopping. You should find that your creative side takes over, and ideas come more easily.

12. Organising your revision

Before you start the whole process of revising, take an hour or so and plan ahead; what you are going to revise, and when you are going to do it. Make yourself a timetable and stick to it. You might want to try planning using a Mind Map. Many people use Mind Maps for revising. I tend to use Mind Maps for creating. Mind Maps are great if you want to spark new ideas.

So, draw a Mind Map. Write down your subjects. Write down the days you are going to revise. Decide which days are going to be allocated to which subjects. You may be better breaking the days down into half or even quarter days depending on how much time you have to allocate. Try to find enough time to revise two different subjects in smaller bursts, rather than one long session of one subject. This will prevent your mind becoming stale or bored.

On each of the days you plan to revise, plan to finish two hours before you are due to go to bed. Relaxing and getting a good nights sleep is just as important as studying. On two of the days of the week, plan to finish an hour earlier than usual, in effect three hours before you go to bed. Use this extra hour to relax. Play on your games console, watch some TV, or meet friends. You deserve the reward if you've been working hard, and it will give your mind a break.

Once you have written all of these sections on your Mind Map, turn them into a timetable for the week. Make sure that you give yourself a day off somewhere in there. Now, once you have all the bits in place, including early finishes, day off, and two hour finish before bed time, work out how much time that leaves you to revise. Perhaps two hours revision or so per evening, more if you have the time, and feel you have then energy or need to do more. Listen to what your body is telling you.

Once you have worked that out, you will then need to divide your revision time by the number of subjects you have to revise. That should give you the amount of time you have to commit to your revision.

One of the most important things I have learned in life is the value of preparation. When you're cooking, having all the ingredients prepared and ready to use, in the order in which you are going to use them, makes life so much easier. Doing a bit of painting and decorating, one of my pet hates, is made a bit more bearable if I have all the tools or materials ready in the right order, so that I can get the task finished as soon as possible. The same applies to revision. Being prepared is a fundamentally important part of the success you are about to have. If you're not prepared, you will find that you have to stop and find information you need, or look for pens or books, or you will have to get a drink, or something to eat. All of that will break your concentration and stop you revising.

Keep yourself hydrated. I don't mean with high sugar or caffeine content drinks. These often leave you feeling tired after the initial energy rush has worn off. Water is the best thing to hydrate you. It will enable you to concentrate. Water is a secret weapon in revision.

I found, once I had my preparation sorted out, that I could plough on with revising, and sometimes, I actually got on such a roll with it, that I got far more done than I thought I would.

13. Adapt and prioritise

If by any chance you get a bit behind with your revision, don't worry. Stay in control. Take a look at your timetable and see if you can create spare time to do an extra bit of revision. Be prepared to adapt. Be prepared to sacrifice a small amount of you time to get the job done. Things happen in every day life to throw your plans out. Learning to prioritise work in order of importance is a skill that most employers look for, so revision can also teach you other useful skills other than academic ones.

14. Speed reading

Speed reading is a good skill to develop. I find that if I am having difficulty understanding a subject, speed reading often makes it clearer, simply because reading larger chunks of material allows you get a bigger picture of the subject.

One of the main reasons we are slow at reading is that we vocalise the words, speak them to ourselves, as we read them, even if it is internally. If you can cut that out, your reading speed will improve dramatically. The best way to do it initially, is to put your finger on the page and move it along as quickly as you can, reading the words as your finger points at them. As you practice, you should find that you get faster at reading, and you vocalise the words less and less. Speed reading can save you an enormous amount of time. Give it a try

15. Efficient reading

A couple of other things I would recommend to you. Make sure you make the best use of your time if you are doing any reading or researching. If you know what you are looking for, the best thing to do, is go to the chapter headings or use the index. Don't waste valuable time hunting through the full book. It can be like looking for a needle in a haystack.

If I cannot find the information I need in the index or chapter headings, and I have to hunt through a book, I tend to speed read it first to find the information I need. When I find a paragraph or section I think is important, I'll put one of those little bookmark sticky notes on it. Later, I'll go back and type the notes up from that. Working smart is much more productive than working hard. Be as specific as possible in your information hunt. Hunting through irrelevant material reduces revision time.

Another thing to try, which many of you will already know, is if you listen to music on your headphones while you are reading, it can help you concentrate more. You have to get the balance right. Experiment with the volume. You cannot have the music too loud, but there is definitely a level where reading and concentration is easier. I found I actually became more focussed on my work. Just enough to cut out outside interference, but not enough to be a distraction.

16. Taking notes

One of the most important skills to learn is taking good notes. This will be a skill that you will use time and time again, as you go through your academic, and working life. At work, if you are in a meeting, or learning a new job, the notes you take will help you remember important information.

There are any number of note taking methods you can use. Some people prefer to just write things down in a jumbled mess. Others draw mind maps. Some people don't take notes at all. That wouldn't work for me.

The method I use helps you see information clearly, and also allows you to reduce and organise notes more quickly. More than that, my technique can allow you to remember every note you ever write.

All you need to do, is number your notes consecutively each time you write one. By this, I don't mean give each paragraph a number, or every four or five sentences. I mean give every sentence you write a number. There are a couple of reasons for this. When I used to write notes and not number them, I found that I just ended up with a mass of writing. Trying to find specific information when I came to revision, meant wading through it all again until I found it. Even when writing my notes, it was much easier to say "refer back to note X", if I wanted to connect several points.

Numbering each point individually, gives each note the same weight as every other note. Every note is important initially. When you go through your notes later, you can throw out the bits you don't want. If you are trying to gain as much information as possible during the lesson, you don't want to be distracted by deciding which notes are important and which are not. Editing your notes later, will also help you understand and absorb what you learned during the lesson.

I would really recommend typing your notes up as soon as you get home after your lesson. Not only will it give you a reminder of what you did in class, but typing them up makes it so much easier when you come to revise. When your notes are typed up, you don't have to worry about writing everything out again. Just cutting and pasting your notes makes editing easier, and allows you to get to the keyword stage much more quickly. That will save you time if you are under pressure nearer the exam. Most word processing software has an outline list you can click on, so that the numbers are added as you enter your notes.

17. Reducing your notes

Fully formed sentences are not easy to remember. What we want to do is to simplify the words so we end up with a set of key words for each sentence. Once you have typed up your notes from class, go through them about a week later. Get rid of all the words that don't do anything other than join the sentences together. Keep only important words. You may have to do this two or three times, but don't fret about it. This is actually part of the process of memorising. The fact that you are reducing the sentences down, helps you to look at the notes in more detail, so you can decide what to keep and what not to. What we want to end up with, is the minimum number of words that mean something to you.

For example, during one class, I wrote, "Question is not whether an act is right or wrong, but whether an act is virtuous." When I edited the note down the first time, I reduced it to, "Not whether act is right or wrong, but whether virtuous." As I looked at my notes again nearer the exam, I reduced it to "Not whether act is right or wrong, whether virtuous." In the last rewrite, I got it down to, "Not right or wrong, whether virtuous." The keywords I want to remember here are: "Not", "Right", "Wrong", "Virtuous".

Once you have edited your notes, leave them a few days. Then re-edit them again, and re-edit again, if you need to. If you are short of time, you can go from the longest version of your notes, to the shortest version, the keywords, but if you have time, do three or four rewrites of each note. It will help it soak into your memory.

18. Breaking down your subject

If you have a problem, say with your computer or your car, you wouldn't sit thinking, there's nothing I can do about it. The chances are you would try, by a process of elimination, to try and narrow the problem down to the possible causes. When you are fairly sure what the cause of the problem is, that is when you stand most chance of being able to fix it. The same thing applies during exams.

Even in the exam itself, if you come across something that you had not prepared for, or simply forgotten, try not to think that you can't solve the problem. The chances are you can. You just have to approach the problem from a different angle. Step back a bit, and think, what is it that I do know, or what am I certain of? When you have decided those things, then bracket them in your mind, and try to concentrate on what's left. Try and break that problem down into even smaller sections. By doing this, although you might not get to a complete answer, you may well pick up marks for what you do know. Breaking the problem down further, chips away at it, and you may well find that at the end of it, the answer is obvious.

19. Don't like your subject? Do this.

There are bound to be subjects you don't like. It's only natural. We are all individuals and we are all drawn to different things. When you are older you get to make choices, but at school or college, you may find you are studying subjects that you cannot get on with.

The first thing to do, is break the subject down, as we did in the previous section with a problem we were presented with. Try and use some thinking time to isolate what it is about the subject that you really don't like. By putting to one side the things you are okay with, and concentrating on what is left, you may be able to isolate why this particular subject does not appeal to you. When you have isolated the problem, have a word with your teacher. The chances are they will be pleased you have taken an interest enough to get to the bottom of the problem, and will be only too happy to help. People love to share what they know, and teachers are no different, especially when someone shows an interest in a subject they may well be passionate about.

One of the reasons for your difficulty, may be, that you don't see the relevance of the subject. Do yourself a favour, and once or twice a week, sit and watch the news on the television, or even pay a visit to the BBC news website. Watch local news programmes to see issues are affecting your local community. As you watch, think about how your lessons relate to the news. You may well find that the problems in the Middle East can be related to something you are learning in history or religious studies. News on the economy may well relate to Maths or Economics, but may also be part of your General Studies or Social Studies. What you should discover is that what you are learning in school is hugely related to the wider world. Once you are able to make a connection, you may well find that you are interested to know more.

There are other possible reasons why you don't like a particular subject. Do you blame your teacher for not making the subject easily understandable for you? You wouldn't be on your own. We have all done it at one time or another. However, your teacher actually has a much harder job than appears on the surface.

We all learn in different ways. Some of us are more drawn to visual ways of learning. Visual examples help us take things in easier. For other people, sound is their preferred route to learning. They are quite happy to listen while someone explains verbally what is going on. Someone who reacts to audio more than visual, might find recording their notes and playing them back might help them to revise. I didn't work for me. I recorded all my notes, which took a long while, switched on the tape, and had to give up within five minutes, because I couldn't stand the sound of my own voice!

The chances of anyone teaching us in exactly the way that we prefer to learn is virtually impossible. Your teacher may have a preference for explaining things a certain way. They will have developed their way of teaching because of the sort of learning preferences they themselves have.

Now imagine how difficult it is, if a teacher has to teach a class with all of these different learning styles. It's no surprise that some subjects may not appeal to you as much as others. Nevertheless, you need to have in mind that everything you learn is important, whether you like, or are interested in the subject, or not. Even the subjects you don't like, may actually help you pass your exams in other subjects. By learning as much as you can about a wide range of subjects, you increase your chances of being able to use information which crosses over from one subject to another.

What your teacher is particularly skilled at, is teaching a subject so that it appeals to the maximum number of people in the class. If you happen to be the one person who doesn't connect with the subject, it may not be your fault, and it is unlikely to be your teacher's either. So what can you do about it?

20. Pro active learning

The first thing to do is take good notes. Taking notes means you have to concentrate on what is being taught. When you get home, read through your notes. See if things appear to make more sense, and are easier to understand.

Try reading information from other another source; books from the library for instance. See if the information is communicated in a way you understand more easily. Some of the greatest minds were amongst the poorest writers, when it came to explaining themselves. Some Philosophers were so technically minded, or their method of explaining their subject so complex, that modern Philosophers are still trying to decipher them centuries later. By hunting around and finding other sources, including online sources, you may find that you find a renewed interest in the subject.

Talk about the subject with friends who enjoy the subject, or with parents. A different perspective can sometimes throw a bit of light on a subject and make that all important difference.

If you can, try and read about your subject before you go to the lesson. Arrive at the lesson with something that you particularly want to find out. Even if you don't naturally have an interest in a subject, try and imagine that you do, and that it is important to you. Use some of the imagination techniques we learned earlier. Imagine yourself being really interested in your subject. If you can find a way to make a connection with a subject, however small, you will find you will pick it up more easily.

21. Memory and recall

Exams are about knowledge and they're about memory. The ability to recall information, sometimes lots of it, when you need it. Some of you may already have come across various forms of the techniques I am going to describe. I've added one or two adaptations which I hope you'll find useful. Learning these techniques should mean that you need never worry about going blank in an exam ever again.

The simple fact is, that humans were never designed for written words. If you think about it, we evolved from mainly visual and hearing animals. We evolved from a fish like creature, which evolved into a rat like mammal, which became a small monkey type mammal. This mammal evolved into apes, and then humans. I know one or two people who didn't evolve very much from the rat like mammal!

Human like creatures go back about eight million years. Modern human beings are about two hundred thousand years old. Humans developed speech about 50,000 years ago. Writing developed about five thousand years ago. So, before we developed speech, in order to memorise anything, we would use our senses and instincts. Most likely, humans relied on visual memory.

Scientists have been working with chimpanzees, to test their recall ability. One particular nine year old chimpanzee, easily out performed humans on visual memory. They had the chimpanzee look at a pattern of images on a screen for just a brief few seconds, and the chimpanzee was able to remember all of them, while the humans taking part in the experiment, barely managed a quarter. Visual memory is part of our evolution.

Having a good memory in the time of the Greeks and Romans was seen as a mark of high intellect. Socrates, the father of philosophy, never wrote anything down. We only know about him from the students who were taught by him. The Greeks and Romans developed memory systems to remember vast amounts of material. The Greek poet Simonides attended a banquet of two thousand people. When he left the room, to talk to two men who wished to speak with him, the roof fell in, killing everyone. They only way anyone knew who was there, was that Simonides had memorised the name of everybody as they came in, and could link them to their position at the dinner table. Xerxes, a warrior king of Persia, could remember the names of all of his twenty thousand men. These ancient techniques are mentioned in probably ninety five per cent of all memory training books. The reason is simple. They work.

There are two secrets to having a good memory. One is having the ability to picture images in your mind. The other, is to be able to fix that image to something. A memory is like a balloon. If you don't fasten it to something, it floats away. There is an old saying, "a picture paints a thousand words." As we shall see, pictures will help you remember far more than a thousand words. This next section may not seem relevant initially, but bear with me. It will give you the basic idea for memorising information. We'll then move on to how to apply it to academic work.

22. Memorising lists

Imagine your Mum says, 'Can you pop to the shops quickly. They close soon, and I desperately need some things for tomorrow.' She starts to reel off a list, but you can't find paper and pen, and you can't text yourself the list, because your phone is out of charge. What do you do? You can try and memorise it, but as the list gets longer and longer, you know you'll miss things off. Let's say your mum asks you to get:

Milk
Bread
Sugar
Washing Up Liquid
Tomatoes
Cucumber
Birthday Card
Tin of beans
Bar of Chocolate
Bathroom Cleaner

So, what do you do? You use your imagination, and turn your body into a giant notepad. Close your eyes, and imagine you have a bottle of milk on your head. Better still, imagine you have a cow sitting on your head. Concentrate on that image, for about six seconds. Next, imagine on your right shoulder, is a loaf of bread, or if you prefer, imagine your shoulder between two slices of bread. See the image in your mind. Now move on to the sugar. Imagine in the crook of your arm, you are trying to balance a bag of sugar. See the sugar spilling out of the bag.

Let's think about the washing up liquid. Imagine on the floor is a bowl of water with some soaps suds and plates in it. Now imagine you are washing plates and cups with your right knee. I know it's bizarre, but get that image in your mind. Imagine you can smell the fragrance of the washing up liquid. Is it citrus or apple? Feel the damp patch on the knee of your jeans. On your right foot, imagine you are juggling a couple of tomatoes. See them jumping into the air as you juggle between one and the other. These bizarre images will help you remember what is on the list.

I'll leave your to create images for the remaining items on the list. Memorise them using the left side of your body. If you decide to replace these items with other ones later, try and remember to go anti-clockwise. That enables you to maintain a system. As you get more confident, you can alter things as you please.

The important thing is that you get the idea that you create an image and attach it to something. That combination of image and place is the basis for good memory. The images you create need to be as unusual as possible. Your brain is excited by the unusual, and often ignores the usual. It is another good reason to keep teaching yourself new things. Your brain is a complex organ which gets bored easily. The more you give it to think about, the happier it is.

You get the idea. Linking the list to something makes it more memorable. Also, remember how we made each image as ridiculous possible.

Okay, so you now know how to create a list. On it's own, that's not going to help you in an exam. Before we move on to the next step though, pause for a minute. You managed to memorise ten bits of information by linking images to your body. You could remember much more. What if you are a fan of a five man band, and you know all their names. Imagine each of them carrying ten items balanced on their head or shoulders and so on. That's fifty items you could remember. If you are a football fan and you know the names of your team, you can remember even more. You could use the team, the substitutes, or even the players from the other teams in the division. Think of the huge list of things you could remember.

Remember, the way this all works is by making the images of what you want to remember, as absurd and exaggerated as possible. Make your images bigger, more colourful. Turn them into cartoons. Have movement in them. If possible, try and imagine smells and sounds. Use your other senses, as well as visual imagery to implant the image into your memory. Provided what you have conjured up is itself unusual and striking, it will come back to you.

The Greeks and the Romans improved this simple system, and their ideas will form the basis of how you will remember huge amounts of information. The Greeks came up with a system call the Loci or place system, and the Roman version of it was the Roman Room or Memory Palace. The Loci version describes how you place what you want to remember along your route or journey. It could be as simple as your journey to school.

Along the route you place the images you have imagined. Let's use the shopping list again. So, you might place an image of a cow at the end of your path. The next one might be a huge loaf of bread at the corner of the street. The next one is a big bag of sugar spilling on to your friends house, or you at the bus stop standing in a huge bowl of washing up liquid, and so on. You simply remember what is in a particular place. If you play computer games, you could even design your own route from scratch. Instead of bad guys leaping out to attack you, you could be surprised by images of your exam revision. Let your imagination run riot, but be sure to make sure that you can recreate the exact route every time you enter it.

The Roman Room is similar, but you place your images around your room. We'll have a go at doing that shortly. Some memory champions have many journeys permanently stored in their memories. Dominic O'Brien who was the world memory champion eight times, has a hundred of these journeys. Fifty of these routes he uses for things he wants to remember permanently, the other fifty for new things. There is no reason why you can't do the same.

In practice, there is little difference between the Loci system or the Roman Room, but you may well find, as I did, that you prefer one more than the other. I preferred the Roman Room version simply because the close proximity of images allowed me to link some images together. It's a matter of personal taste. Some people prefer to go further than this, and break down some of the objects in their room. For instance, if you have a radio in your room, you could place items you want to remember on the volume control, on the tuning dial, the handle, aerial, and so on. It will depend on how much information you have to memorise, and what your personal preferences are.

When you've have worked out your route, and your connections to the information at each point on the journey, try it out a few times. You need to make sure that the connection between image and information is strong. In one exam, I managed to create a good image to remember someone's name, but not a strong enough connection to tell me what her actual quote was. Sometimes that can happen if you have been rushing to get things done. Take the extra few seconds to make sure you have a good connection. Test it regularly. The great thing about the Roman Room or the Loci system is that you can go back and forward along the route, and because the visual images and connections are so strong, you can interchange the order of the information you write. So, when you are in an exam, you can decide which order to write things, in order to create the best answer to the question.

23. Memorising difficult words

Images are key to helping you remember. However, you might find that some words are not that easy to turn into an image. Break longer words down into smaller ones. Take a word like "Psychology". If you knew what Sigmund Freud looked like, it might allow you to remember the word, but you could also imagine Psy, the guy who sang "Gangnam style", dancing about with an American college jumper on, perhaps even dressed as a cheerleader. In effect, Psy + collegy.

As another example, let's use our note from section 17, the word "virtuous". The word virtuous is slightly awkward. We could use the phrase "chew us" to represent the second half of the word. If we add the word "fur" to it, we can imagine "fur" + "chew us", and there we have the phrase "fur chew us", which sounds a bit like virtuous. I can imagine us being attacked by a wolf who is chewing big chunks out of us. Imagine the pain, or how scared we are, and I think we have a pretty effective image

24. Using people as memory aids

I have always been fascinated by people, so for me, using people, alive or dead, as a memory aid can be useful. People can often represent a whole country or organisation. During one exam, I had to remember the Philosopher St. Anselm. The word Anselm sounded a bit like handsome, and so I remembered his name by using George Clooney to represent the word handsome. God is represented in many areas of history, as well as religion, and the best person I found to represent God, was my father. Images of people are as useful as cartoons or other visual images. There's a huge variety to choose from, so take your pick.

25. Actor or musician?

Another technique worth mentioning is learning by rote or repetition. Now that may seem like the boring side of revision that you've tried to avoid. I have to admit I used to think that, until I learned to use it properly. If there is not too much to learn, I'll us it in addition to the Roman Room method, simply as a back up. It is worth getting to know how to do it, just in case it suits your learning style.

Actors and musicians tend to learn lines or music by this method. They learn a short section, go back to the beginning and play or recite it again. When they are sure they know the first piece, they will add the next section to it. They'll go back to the beginning and play or recite those two sections until they know them off by heart, and when they do, they add the next piece, and so on.

You can do this with your notes. Learn a section by repetition, and then add another and another, until you can remember the whole piece. You should be able to remember about five hundred words in about two and a half hours. However, rather than simply sitting down and doing this, it is better if you can, to walk around your room, at a steady pace. This gets the blood and the oxygen flowing, and aids the retention of information. This is why you often see students reading the Kuran or the Talmud rocking back and forwards. Movement aids memory.

26. Memorise all your notes.

You remember I mentioned there was another reason to number the notes you take? Here's why.

Dominic O'Brien, introduced a system which turned the first ten letters of the alphabet into the numbers one to ten (although zero was used instead of ten).

A=1	B=2	C=3
D=4	E=5	F=6

G=7	H=8	I=9
J=0

Now if you look at your notes and decide that you want to remember note number 42. That gives you the letters DB. Know anyone with those initials? David Beckham perhaps? What about note 88 or HH. Harry Hill? So, for instance, if one of your parents had a credit card with the pin number 4288, and needed help to remember the number, they could simply turn the numbers into letters, and think of David Beckham standing next to Harry Hill. To reinforce the combination even further, think of David Beckham wearing Harry Hill's big collar and glasses, and Harry Hill playing football against him. That makes the image even stronger.

Converting numbers to letters in this way is ideal for remembering historical dates, time of the day, or elements of the periodic table, amongst other things.

This is the sort of technique that scientists use if they want to show off by writing Pi to huge numbers of decimal places. Changing numbers to letters, means that you can then make up words or mnemonics to help them remember. We all know mnemonics like Richard of York gave battle in vain, to remember the colours of the rainbow, red, orange, green, blue, indigo, violet. Mnemonics are great for small specific bits of information.

So, let's go back to note 42. Imagine, for example, you were studying Geography. What you could do is imagine David Beckham sitting on a globe. All you would have to do then is link the actual note you have written, to the image of David Beckham sitting on a globe.

Say for note number 42, we wrote:
"The Great Pyramid of Giza is the oldest and largest of the three pyramids in the Giza Necropolis, Egypt".

To make it easier to remember, we might reduce it to:

" Great Pyramid Giza > oldest and largest of 3 pyramids in Giza Necropolis > Egypt" (I use > to separate bits of sentences, rather than commas or full stops > it seems to make the notes easier to read).

Have a look at the reduced note. Can we reduce it any further? I don't think so. So how are we going to make it memorable?

The main keywords are: "Great Pyramid Giza", "oldest and largest", "3 pyramids", "Giza Necropolis", "Egypt".

We could imagine a pyramid monster with a cockney accent, called the Great Pyramid geezer. Or, you could imagine a huge live pyramid with a water spout or geyser shooting out of his head. I'm going to go with the first idea, because I can imagine this huge old Pyramid geezer standing next to two other pyramids, one smaller than the other. You could imagine all three pyramids with arms and legs. The Great Pyramid of Giza has a walking stick to exaggerate the "old" part of the note. That takes care of: "Great Pyramid Giza > oldest and largest of 3 pyramids". What about "in Giza Necropolis?"

For the necropolis part, split the word up. Let's imagine, neck, crop and police. Imagine another cockney geezer with a crop of wheat coming out of his neck, and wearing a police helmet or a flashing blue light. Use the sound of the word to create an image, not necessarily the way the word is spelt.

For the "in Egypt" part, we can easily imagine a fez as an image to represent Egypt.

So, originally note number 42 in your Geography notes read:

"The Great Pyramid of Giza is the oldest and largest of the three pyramids in the Giza Necropolis, Egypt".

To represent that, we've turned it into a huge old pyramid geezer, standing next to two smaller pyramid people, each smaller than the other. The second pyramid geezer has a crop of wheat sticking out of his neck, and a fez with a blue light on the top. If you imagine that the geezer with the fez with the blue light is David Beckham who is sitting on a globe, you can get some idea of how it all links together. That is just one example of one note. You may find within your list of notes that there are other links which will enable even greater possibilities for creating images to join everything together and make them more memorable

Think of those images and see how they represent our original note. Now this is just my example. You will find your own ideas are much more memorable. Check back and forward between image and note to make sure the image reminds you of the note. If not, make changes which are more memorable. Imagine a note you have written for number 88. When you have the note image certain in your mind, you could, if you wish, link it with Harry Hill sitting on a globe. If you followed the same process with each one of your notes, there is a good chance that you could remember every single one of them. You could even combine this with the Loci or Roman Room technique to fix the information in place. There are a number of websites which provide lists of celebrity name suggestions for each letter of the alphabet.

27. Another example

Let's do a Roman Room example. Here are some reduced notes I wrote for an exam question on dealing with world hunger:

1) World hunger > what are our obligations to help?
2) O'Neill > could figure out moral framework
3) Need to work out what a good framework is
4) How often does it get things right?
5) How often does it tell us what to do?
6) Utilitarian approach > max utility > highest for all people
7) How well off would people be > cannot do calculation
8) Could make everyone better off
9) Utilitarianism would say feed better off and not feed worse off
10) McMahon > we don't need framework > we don't have for morality

To memorise these notes, I want you to imagine a square living room. You are standing in the living room doorway looking straight ahead. To your left is a three seater settee. Next to the settee is a side table with a reading lamp on it. Opposite you, underneath the main window, is a two seater settee.

On the right hand wall is a sideboard with three things on it, a lamp, an ornament of a man, and an mp3 player. Next to that, the fireplace with a large mirror above it. The chances are, for such a small amount of information, we won't need to use all of this room, but I hope it gives you some idea of picking out easily recognisable objects to use as memory points.

We'll go clockwise. On the first seat of the three seater settee, to represent note 1) from the above list, I am going to imagine an image of a starving African child who is holding his hands out asking for help. In front of the child, I am going to imagine myself with a big question mark over my head. I am standing on the back of an alligator, because the sound of the word alligator reminds me slightly of obligation. It is not a pleasant image, but is a memorable one. No-one can read your mind. As long as your images are memorable to you, whatever they may be, that is all you need to concern yourself with. For the moment, we are simply concerned with you getting the best marks possible.

Moving to note 2), we move to the second seat on the three seater settee. Here I am going to imagine Martin O'Neill, the football manager. He has a bishop's hat on his head, which, because it is an unusual image, will remind me of the word moral. Around his hat, he has a wooden framework (note 3). As he sits there, I imagine the starving child reaching over and asking, 'How often does it get things right?' (note 4). I imagine the framework around the bishop's hat, suddenly sprouting a finger and wagging it at me, pointing and telling me what to do (note 5).

That means, in the space of two seats, I have memorised notes 1) to 5) already.

For note 6): On the third seat, I am going to imagine someone dressed in a military uniform. Military sounds vaguely similar to utilitarian. The next phrase is max utility, so I am going to imagine a Pepsi max balanced on the head of a meter reader from the Gas company, which is a utility company. I'm then going to imagine the military man and the gas man jumping up on the back of the settee, as though climbing a hill, where they find lots of people at the top.

Next we move to the table, next to the three seater settee, for note 7). Here I imagine a red Indian sitting crossed legged on top of the table lamp with his hand raised saying, 'How'. Indians always seemed to say 'How' in the old cowboy films. He is staring at a calculator and shaking his head. The red Indian looks down into a deep well, drops the calculator, and then raises his other hand in which he's holding a red card, as though sending someone off.

We are now using the two seater settee under the window. Note number 8) has the least words, but is harder to create an image for. Let's imagine lots of people jumping up and down in celebration throwing money into the air. On the next seat along, I imagine another man in a military uniform, (note 9) a different uniform though. The military man is pushing food towards the people who are celebrating, and encouraging them to eat. He is holding his other hand up in front of some poor looking people, as though telling them they will not be fed.

For note 10), we'll move to the sideboard. I imagine Vince McMahon from WWE, the wrestling programme, standing on top of the lamp on the sideboard. He is destroying a similar framework to the one on Martin

O'Neill's hat. The ornament of a man, which stands next to the table lamp has another bishop's hat on his head. MacMahon snatches it from the ornaments head and throws it to the ground, which reminds me that we don't have a framework for morality.

That's it. I'm sure you will agree it is absolute nonsense, but it is memorable nonsense. What I would do now is go back over the images I have created, and check how memorable they are. For instance on note 1), I can clearly remember the starving child, and me stood on the alligator, but the question mark is not sticking, so I might need to change that. I might actually turn my head into a question mark. It does not take very long to create these nonsense images, but you then need to spend a few minutes checking that the image does indeed remind you of what it is you are trying to memorise.

28. Past papers

Some people like to have a trial run and answer past papers. If you feel confident that might help, then by all means do it. Past papers are not for everyone. Like running a race too close to a main event, you might find that you peak too soon, and in some cases, it may affect your confidence. Try it and see. If it does not work, don't do it again next time. The important thing is to try and reach a peak of performance on the day of the exam.

If your school or college require you to do mock exams, use the experience to get used to this system of memorising information. Hopefully, your success will give you confidence when it comes to your exams. However, it will also allow you to highlight what does not work well, and adapt for your real exams.

Listen out for hints from teachers. They sometimes give information away, even when they don't mean to. I knew a particular subject was a favourite of a lecturer of mine, judging by how many times he would refer to it during a lecture. Surprise, surprise, there it was on the exam paper. However, you should not try to gamble. If you think you may know some of what is coming up on the paper, just use it as a bit of detailed information. Don't neglect parts of your revision because you think they might not come up. Exams are not the best place to take risks.

29. Panic stations!

So, you've left it too late, eh? The fact is, that even if you leave your revising until late, it is still possible to pass your exams. There is little point worrying what might have been. If you keep a clear head, it may still not be too late.

You can review your exam approach prior to revising for your next exam. Learn from any mistakes then. In the meantime, you still have an exam to pass.

If you've left it late, then the techniques we have talked about can still work, as long as you have a reasonable understanding of your subject. That understanding will have come from the work you did in class, plus any homework you might have done. The revision techniques we have talked about don't replace what you know, they just help you to recall it when you need it. I managed to pass my first exam using these techniques by learning them a fortnight before. In my case, I had done the work in class and at home, and my weak area was simply being able to recall information in the exam.

Before you do any last minute revision, take an hour or so to plan what you can do in the remaining time before the exam. Work smart. Think about what you already know. Once you have identified your strong points, you need to decide what the other areas are where you might pick up marks. Concentrate on those areas first of all. If you manage to leave yourself enough time, go on to what you regard as your weakest parts of the subject next.

Leave just enough time to quickly revise your strong points, so you have the information locked solid.

With more time, you would probably start revising areas where most work needs to be done first of all, and finish with the areas where you need least work. Even if you do start revising late, it is well worth planning in terms of what you can achieve in a shorter space of time. You can still be organised and prioritise. Be positive, and you might still surprise yourself!

30. The day of the exam

Treat the exam as though you were an athlete ready for the hundred metres final, or a boxer about to go into the ring. Focus. Try not to talk to other people about the exams. Once, before an exam, I was standing near someone who started talking about part of a subject that I had not revised. I heard this, and started to panic. When I went into the exam, my head was so full of this bit of the subject, that it wiped out everything else. What made it worse was that the subject didn't even come up anyway. Forget other people, and just concentrate on what you've revised. At the end of the day, if you have revised well for a particular part of the subject and it doesn't come up in the exam, if you stay calm, you might be able to use some other knowledge or some of the information you have revised for another question.

When you find your seat, sit down and try and relax. Breathe slowly and gently. Have a sip of water. Take a look around and familiarise yourself with your surroundings. Put your watch on the desk to help keep track of the time. Take things nice and easy. When you get the nod to turn the paper over, take your time, relax and read through all the questions thoroughly. Read what the questions actually ask, not what you hope they ask. Read through them a second time. When you are sure which ones you want to answer, have another good read of the question. What <u>exactly</u> are they asking? What are the important words in the question? Every word in an exam question usually has significance, so underline the words which state what is required. When you have done that, take a minute or two to think about the route or room, where you linked your information. Either relax and get your thoughts together, take a sip of water, or if you feel confident, start to write.

If you know which questions are likely to pick up the most marks, then answer those as soon as possible. Leaving the question which may give you the most marks, might leave you vulnerable to running out of time. Get the points in the bag. It's all about the scores on the doors.

You should already know how much time is required for each question. Your teachers may already have mentioned it to you. Perhaps you may already have taken mock exams. Keep to your allocated time, if possible. You may find that you are on a roll on a particular subject you know well, and feel the urge to keep going, but remember, it may reduce the time you have for the next question.

If your mind goes blank in the exam, don't think about the information you are trying to remember. Think about your room, or your journey. Where did you place the information in it. What was next to it? You should find that thinking about the room and the images, rather than the information you are trying to remember, will make things come back to you much more easily. Even if you don't recall the image and information you need straight away, but you know roughly where it is, by going back and forward, say between two pieces of furniture, you should find that the information you are seeking miraculously springs into your head.

Staying calm is much more likely to bring the information back to you, rather than panic. Slow your breathing down. Take a sip of water. Recall the image. If you can't, don't worry. Come back to it later. Remember what we said earlier about breaking the problem down into smaller pieces, trying to isolate the information you need.

31. Forget it!

When the exam is over, forget it. Don't beat yourself up if you missed something. There is nothing you can do once you have left the room, so why worry? If it is your final exam, then treat yourself. Even if you have other exams to do, take some time to allow yourself to wind down. Relax. Watch a film, or spend some time on your games console or with friends. Take time out to celebrate the fact that it is over.

It can be worth keeping some kind of study diary or notebook. Perhaps even write notes on your exam timetable. Write down anything that worked really well during your revision, or make a note of anything that your really want to avoid next time you take an exam.

32. If…

James Hetfield, of the band Metallica, has a tattoo which says "live to win, dare to fail". He's right. It is okay to fail. Failure is not what we aspire to, but we learn just as much, if not more, from our failures as much as our successes. Learning what not to do, is just as important as learning what we should do. Finding out what we don't like, is as important as learning what we do. Many top authors, actors and pop stars have made it to the top after many years of failure and struggle. Top business people have often failed more than once, before they hit on the idea that brings them success. Even in relationships, it is often the case that we meet the right person after we have one or two failed relationships. Failure is every bit as important as being successful. It's just a different way of learning, and not necessarily the worst way to learn either

If things do go wrong, it's not the end of the world. The chances are there will be other chances of one kind or another at which you will excel. You might be upset for a few hours, but think about what the worst thing that could ever happen to you, and you'll find that not achieving the marks you want in an exam is not even in the top ten. Also, think about me. Go on, force yourself. I was fifty four years old when I went to university. Some of us are just late developers. We are Opsimaths; someone who learns later in life.

There is no doubt that if you can achieve as much as possible earlier in your life, then doors open earlier for you. That applies whether you take exams, or an apprenticeship, or some other work. In the long run, you are likely to get greater rewards if you build on what you achieve when you are younger, rather than trying to do it when you are older. However, don't forget that life is just a series of random episodes. You can guarantee that when you have overcome one problem, there will be another one along soon for you to deal with. It is how you deal with problems that makes life bearable. The main thing is to try and retain as much control as you can over any situation. If you are in control of your own destiny as much as possible, then you are the person who will make the decisions. If you don't have control, someone will make those decisions for you. That does not mean you shouldn't compromise. Hopefully, if common sense prevails, everyone involved should feel happy about the outcome of any situation. At the end of the day, what matters more than anything is happiness. For you, your friends and your family.

I hope that what you have learned over the past hour or so will remove some of the fear of exams. As I discovered the hard way, there is a strategy to revising, and many students don't have that knowledge. You do. So make the most of it. I would wish you good luck, but somehow I don't think you'll need it.

APPENDIX 1

Maths

Memorising equations

Have a look at this equation. To memorise something like this, I would be tempted to make up a story

$$\frac{F1 + F2 - t/n \; F1F2}{1 - t/n \; F2}$$

For example, Fabio and Fergie take Thandie Newton to see Franz Ferdinand on the top floor. On the floor below, someone takes Thandie Newton to see Fergie.

We could also memorise the operators; the plus, minus, division and multiplication signs. I have adopted the red cross symbol for a plus sign. For a minus sign. I have opted for a pizza, a takeaway pizza, because another way of expressing minus is take away. Likewise, I imagine the pizza cutter dividing the pizza. For multiplying, I decided on an image of Simon Cowell, because he reminds me of the X Factor.

Imagine Fabio and Fergie with Red cross labels on their sleeves. Then imagine Thandie Newton carrying a pizza, a takeaway pizza, going to see Franz Ferdinand. Franz Ferdinand have an oversize pizza cutter in their hands, because they are going to divide something. Someone, takes Thandie Newton to see Fergie. That someone is Simon Cowell.

To memorise the equation, you will need to put the operator signs in the correct position. This is actually easier to do than describe on paper. Use your imagination to imprint the image into your memory banks

Trigonometry

In Trigonometry, we used to remember the relationship between Tangent Cosine, and Sine by the phrase:

        The   Cat   Sat
        On   An   Orange
        And   Howled Horribly

Which represented:

Tangent	Cosine	Sine
Opposite	Adjacent	Opposite
Adjacent	Hypotenuse	Hypotenuse

I found it easier to imagine someone tangoing opposite Jason Bourne, which translates to tangent equals opposite over adjacent. The costume on Jason's hippo was easier to remember than Cosine equals Adjacent over Hypotenuse. I could Imagine a road sign showing an Operation on a Hippo, better than Sine equals Opposite over Hypotenuse.

Processes

You can also use the techniques we have learned so far, to try and set in our mind the mathematical processes we might need to use. You know what it's like, you start solving an equation, and then cannot remember what to do next. Rather than try to remember the process by repetition, although there is nothing wrong with that, see if you can create a story around the process of solving equations. Make sure your process is correct before you start to memorise it.

For example, if we have the equation: $5x - 4 = 3(x + 2)$, how would you go about solving it?

You might say, multiply what's in the brackets by 3 first of all.

That would give you, $\qquad 5x - 4 = 3x + 6$.

We could get rid of the 3x by taking it from both sides which would leave,

$$2x - 4 = 6$$

Take the − 4 over to the other side of the equals sign to leave the 2x on its own. As it crosses over it becomes a + 4, so we end up with 2x = 6 +4, so

$$2x = 10$$

Therefore $x = 5$

In order to explain what steps we took to solve the equation, we could say: we multiplied the bracket; we simplified the equation by bringing together similar terms; we divided both sides by the number of xs. If you were in an exam, could you remember the various steps in the right order?

In order to remember the process, we could go back to our Roman Room idea. In effect we have three key phrases to remember from the process:
   a) Multiply the bracket,
   b) Bring together similar terms,
   c) Divide both sides by the number of xs.

This time we'll use the kitchen. As you walk into the kitchen; on the left hand side, there is a microwave, a toaster and a kettle.

For the first part a), like we did in the equation example, we are using the image of Simon Cowell as the symbol for multiplication. Imagine him with a racquet (to represent brackets) pinging out of the microwave.

Next for b), we can conjure up an image of bell ringers, ringing together, as the Olsen twins, wearing graduation gowns pop up out of the toaster. The Olsen twins remind us of the word similar, while the graduation gowns remind us of school terms.

Finally, we could imagine two X Factor winners, say James Arthur and Leona Lewis, both with pizza cutters in their hands, cutting through our kettle. That gives us dividing both sides by the number of Xs. We can't use Simon Cowell to represent x in this case, because he already represents the symbol for multiplication.

The chances are that most Maths students would use BODMAS, Brackets of Division, Multiplication, Addition, Subtraction. That tells us in which order we should approach an equation in terms of its operators, but doesn't tell us what to do with the equation in terms of how we go about using BODMAS. This is where our memory techniques are useful.

Once again, you may well be able to come up with more memorable images, but I have simply chosen these to illustrate that you can remember processes, as well as information. This technique may be useful if you wanted to memorise a Chemistry process, or even in work, if you are dismantling a car, or even memorising the process of cutting hair correctly. The great thing is, as the route or room points are fixed, if you have to, you can reverse the process. If you had learned how to take a part of a car apart, you can put it back together again, by taking the reverse route.

APPENDIX 2

Memorising songs

One of my hobbies is playing guitar. I'm not brilliant, but it's something I enjoy. Learning an instrument is a great way of taking your mind off things. The problem was, that I believed my memory was so bad, that I never got around to learning any songs, so I used to make up my own. I can play chords, but half the time could never remember their names or play them in the right order to learn a song. However, using the techniques I have been describing, I've come up with a system that works for me.

First of all I named the major chords after a famous figure:

A = Adolf,
B = Bono,
C = Churchill,
D = Diana,
E = Einstein,
F = Fidel
G = Gandhi.

For minor chords, I use:

A minor = Andy Murray
B minor = Bob Marley
C minor = Chris Martin
D minor = Dean Martin
E minor = Ewan Macgregor
F minor = Freddie Mercury
G minor = George Michael.

If I want to add a sharp to the chord, I simply imagine the person with a pointed head, and if I want to add a flat, I imagine them with a flat head. In addition to this, I can add one of the seven dwarves if the chord is a 7th, and one of the Jackson Five, probably Michael Jackson, if a 5th needs to be added. Augmented usually reminds me of breast implants, so I imagine the characters with large boobs, which reminds me of an augmented chord. That works well seeing as most of the characters are male. For a suspended chord, I can imagine one of my characters hanging upside down from the ceiling.

As nearly all modern songs have lyrics, all I have to do is match up where the chord change is, with the nearest word. For instance, if someone sings, "I love you," and there is a chord change to C at the word "I", I could perhaps imagine Churchill with one huge eye instead of two normal ones. If the chord changed at the work "love", I could imagine Winston Churchill with a big heart on the outside of his coat, or perhaps a gruesome picture with his chest opened up. If the chord change came at the word "you", I would imagine Winston Churchill standing beside a female sheep, a ewe. The image would be enough to remind me to play a C chord when the singer sings "I love you."

This shows the flexibility of the techniques. You are really only limited by your imagination.

Recommended Reading

Becker, L. (2010). 14 Days to Exam Sucess. Basingstoke : Palgrave MacMillan.

Institute, P. (2008). Pelmanism, the forgotten secrets of success. Devox.

Lorayne, H., & Lucas, J. (1974). The Memory Book: The Classic Guide to Improving Your Memory at Work, at School, and at Play. New York: The Ballantine Publishing Group.

O'Brien, D. (2003). How to Pass Exams. London: Duncan Baird Publishers Ltd.

Robbins, A. (1986). Unlimited Power. London: Simon and Schuster Ltd.

Printed in Great Britain
by Amazon